Life in the UK Test
Practice Questions

Questions and answers for
British citizenship & settlement tests

....

Published by Red Squirrel Publishing

Red Squirrel Publishing
Suite 235, 77 Beak Street,
London, W1F 9DB, United Kingdom

www.redsquirrelbooks.com

First edition published in 2006
Second Edition – Fifth Impression

ISBN-10: 0-9552-1593-5
ISBN-13: 978-0-9552-1593-3

Edited by Henry Dillon, Alastair Smith and Erwan Pirou

Designed and artworked by
Cox Design Partnership, Witney, Oxon

Printed in the UK by CPI William Clowes Beccles NR34 7TL

CONTENTS

IMPORTANT INFORMATION

Many of the facts that you need to learn for your test relate to laws and regulations determined and administered by the government. The practice questions in this book are based on materials published by the Home Office in February 2007. Since that time some laws and regulations have changed, meaning that some questions in this book may be out of date.

However, the Home Office advises that your test will ONLY cover published material. You are NOT required to know that a law or regulation has changed.

While these changes to laws and regulations will not be reflected in your test you may be interested to know what they are. An updated list of the changes can be found on our website by visiting **www.lifeintheuk.net/out-of-date**

INTRODUCTION

If you're planning to become a British citizen or apply to live permanently in the UK then taking the Life in the UK Test will be one of your first steps.

Over 100,000 people take the Life in the UK Test every year. Unfortunately, Home Office statistics show that nearly one in three people fail their test. As the test is expensive to sit, and time consuming to study for, it is best that you pass your test first time.

By using this book and studying hard you can approach your test with confidence that you will be one of those who pass the test and go on to make Britain their permanent home.

About this book

This study book is designed to test your knowledge of the official study materials before sitting the Life in the UK Test. It will allow you to assess your progress in learning and understanding the study materials, so that you will know when you are ready to take your official test.

The book is packed with hundreds of practice questions for you to test yourself. Each question is drawn from chapters 2, 3, 4, 5 and 6 of the official Home Office materials. The questions are arranged into 17 tests. The tests and questions are in the same format as the official test.

The book also contains advice on how you should go about your study. Read these sections carefully for tips on how you can study effectively and get maximum value from the practice tests.

Take some time to read through the following sections carefully. They tell you about all the features of this book and will enable you to get as much out of it as possible.

How to prepare for the test

1. Study the materials

All the questions that can be asked in the Life in the UK Test are based on official study materials provided by the Home Office. These are published in a handbook called *Life in the United Kingdom: A Journey to Citizenship* and can also be found in our *Life in the UK Test: Study Guide*. Further details about the study guide can be found at our website **www.lifeintheuk.net**

TIP Before you start your study, note that your official test will only ask questions based on **Chapters 2, 3, 4, 5 and 6** of the Home Office publication. The questions in this book are also drawn **only from those chapters**.

2. Take practice tests

Once you've finished thoroughly reviewing the study materials you should check if you are ready to take the test by completing several practice tests from this book.

There are 17 general practice tests in this book. Each of the practice tests is different and contains 24 unique questions. Each test contains questions covering all parts of the study materials.

When you sit your official test you will be given 45 minutes to complete the test. So when you take a practice test you should allow yourself the same time. The pass mark in the official test is at least 75% – or only six incorrect answers. Again, this is what you should aim to score when you take a practice test.

If you can consistently score at least 75% and finish a test within 45 minutes then you are ready to take your official test.

If you do not pass the practice tests satisfactorily and do not feel confident enough to sit your official test then you should continue your study. If you do not have sufficient time left before your official test to do more study, then you may be able to reschedule your test appointment. Most test centres are happy to do this if you give them reasonable notice. However, there may be a £10 administration fee if you give less than seven days notice. Contact your test centre for more details.

3. Regional tests

Some of the questions asked in your test may be specific to the part of Britain where you are taking your test. If you are taking the test in Scotland, Wales or Northern Ireland then you can check your understanding of questions specific to your respective countries in tests 18–20. Questions relevant to England appear in the general tests 1–17.

4. Test marking

The answers for each test are provided in the back of the book. To make scoring easier, cut out the marking sheet at the back of the book and use this to record your answers.

5. Online tests

Once you've finished testing yourself using the questions in this book, you can go online and access further tests with our free subscription offer.

Visit **www.lifeintheuk.net** to redeem this offer.

WARNING: DO NOT MEMORISE QUESTIONS

The practice questions contained in this book are intended to help you assess your understanding of the study materials and check if you are ready to take the official test.

Do not prepare for the test by memorising the questions in this book.

All the questions are in the same format as the official test questions. But they are not identical to the questions in the official test. The Home Office regularly revises the wording of questions used in the Life in the UK Test.

It is very important that you fully read and understand the study materials before taking your test.

SEND US YOUR FEEDBACK

Our books have helped thousands of people pass the Life in the UK Test. So we're always delighted when we hear from our readers. You can send us your comments by visiting **www.lifeintheuk.net/feedback**

CHECKLIST

There are a lot of things that you need to remember to do for the Life in the UK Test. Avoid problems and get organised by completing this checklist.

☐ Test appointment booked

Book your test by visiting **www.lifeintheuk.net/book** or by calling the Life in the UK Test Helpline on **0800 015 4245**

Test Date   Time

Test Centre Address

Phone

☐ Finished reading study materials

☐ Completed Practice Tests

☐ Completed Free Online Practice Tests

☐ Checked latest tips and advice at **www.lifeintheuk.net**

☐ Valid photographic ID arranged

☐ Test centre location and travel route confirmed

PRACTICE TEST 1

1 When was the Second World War?

    A 1840–1846

    B 1901–1918

    C 1919–1925

    D 1939–1945

2 Which of these statements is correct?

    A Some young people work to pay for their university fees and expenses

    B University education is free to anyone who wishes to study

3 When did married women gain the right to retain ownership of their own money and property?

    A 1752

    B 1792

    C 1810

    D 1882

4 From which two locations did Britain admit refugees during the late 1960s?

    A Ethiopia

    B South East Asia

    C Turkey

    D Uganda

5 What percentage of the UK's population live in England?

    A 53%

    B 68%

    C 75%

    D 84%

6 What is the name of the patron saint of Scotland?

    A St Andrew

    B St David

    C St George

    D St Patrick

7 When is Mother's Day?

    A The Saturday four weeks before Easter

    B The Sunday four weeks before Easter

    C The Sunday one week before Easter

    D The Sunday three weeks before Easter

8 When are general elections held?

    A At least every year

    B At least every four years

    C At least every five years

    D At least every ten years

9 When can a magistrate decide whether a person is guilty or innocent?

    A A magistrate can always decide whether a person is guilty or innocent regardless of the alleged crime

    B A magistrate can not decide whether a person is guilty or innocent; instead a jury must always be used

    C If a person is accused of having committed a minor crime

    D If a person is accused of having committed a serious crime

10 European Union law is legally binding in the UK. Is this statement true or false?

    A True

    B False

11 **What is the main aim behind the European Union today?**

    A For member states to function as a single market

    B For member states to improve efficiency

    C For member states to observe a single set of laws

    D For member states to protect human rights in Europe

12 **Newspapers can not publish political opinions or run campaigns to influence government. Is this statement true or false?**

    A True

    B False

13 **How many member states are there in the Commonwealth?**

    A 25 member states

    B 39 member states

    C 53 member states

    D 75 member states

14 **When did the UK join the European Union?**

    A 1935

    B 1959

    C 1973

    D The UK is not a member of the European Union

15 **Who will provide the legal agreements necessary for you to buy a home?**

    A A bank

    B A solicitor

    C A surveyor

    D The local authority

16 It is not possible to choose between electricity and gas suppliers. Is this statement true or false?

    A True

    B False

17 What do you need to provide to open a bank account? Select two options from below

    A £500

    B A work permit

    C Proof of your address

    D Proof of your identity

18 What is the maximum number of hours that a child can work in any school week?

    A 12 hours

    B 18 hours

    C 20 hours

    D 38 hours

19 What is the speed limit for cars and motorcycles in built-up areas?

    A 30 miles per hour

    B 50 miles per hour

    C 60 miles per hour

    D 70 miles per hour

20 You need an appointment to visit a NHS walk-in centre. Is this statement true of false?

    A True

    B False

21 Schools in the UK that are linked to a particular religion are called 'faith schools'. Is this statement true or false?

   A True

   B False

22 What might you need to complete or provide when applying for a job? Select two options from below

   A An application form or your curriculum vitae

   B A gas or telephone bill

   C A covering letter or letter of application

   D Proof of a bank account

23 Select the correct statement from below

   A If you are self-employed then you need to pay your own tax

   B People that are self-employed have tax automatically taken from their earnings

24 Your employer can dismiss you for being a union member. Is this statement true or false?

   A True

   B False

PRACTICE TEST 2

1 Why was there a fall in the number of people migrating to the UK from the West Indies, India, Pakistan and Bangladesh in the late 1960s?

  A A weak British currency made immigration less appealing

  B It was becoming more difficult for immigrants to find employment in the UK

  C New laws were introduced restricting immigration to Britain

  D These countries were experiencing labour shortages

2 More young people are smoking and, in particular, more girls smoke than boys. Is this statement true or false?

  A True

  B False

3 There are more men in study at university than women. Is this statement true or false?

  A True

  B False

4 During the 1950s, textile and engineering firms from the UK sent recruitment agents to which two countries? Select two countries from below

  A India

  B Pakistan

  C Poland

  D South Africa

5 **According to the 2001 Census, what percentage of the UK population are Christians?**

  A About 50%

  B About 90%

  C About 70% ✗

  D About 20%

6 **When is Christmas celebrated?**

  A 1 January

  B 24 December

  C 25 December

  D 25 November

7 **What is the name of the patron saint of Northern Ireland?**

  A St Andrew

  B St David

  C St George

  D St Patrick ✗

8 **The Prime Minister and most members of the Cabinet are MPs. Is this statement true or false?**

  A True ✗

  B False

9 **What is a quango?**

  A A local police officer

  B A non-departmental public body ✗

  C Another name for the Lord Chancellor

  D The name of the British citizenship ceremony

10 **A country can not be expelled from the Council of Europe.**
Is this statement true or false?

   A True

   B False

11 **What must a candidate have in order to become a local councillor?**

   A A connection with the area in which they wish to take office

   B A deposit of £500

   C A recommendation from their local MP

   D Membership of a political party

12 **Who from the list below is not responsible for**
controlling the finances of the police?

   A Councillors

   B Magistrates

   C Police Ombudsman

   D The Government

13 **If you rent a room in a shared house, and you watch TV**
in your room, you must buy your own separate TV licence.
Is this statement true or false?

   A True

   B False

14 **What are the roles of the Whips in Parliament?**
Select two correct roles from below

   A Responsible for discipline in their party

   B Ensure attendance of MPs at voting time in the House of Commons

   C Ensure the House of Commons is always safe and secure

   D Keep order in the House of Commons during political debates

15 **Who carries out checks on a house that you want to buy?**

    A A housing association

    B A landlord

    C A surveyor

    D A builder

16 **Which phone numbers should be called in an emergency for police, fire and ambulance services? Select two options from below**

    A 999

    B 112

    C 111

    D 911

17 **People have to buy a TV licence for each individual TV they own. Is this statement true or false?**

    A True

    B False

18 **In which year did the NHS begin?**

    A 1911

    B 1939

    C 1948

    D 2000

19 **What is the speed limit for cars and motorcycles on motorways and dual carriageways?**

    A 100 miles per hour

    B 50 miles per hour

    C 60 miles per hour

    D 70 miles per hour

20 **What are you called if you need to stay overnight in hospital?**

   A A day patient

   B A night patient

   C An in-patient

   D An outpatient

21 **Where are children taught Welsh in school?**

   A England

   B Wales

   C Northern Ireland

   D Scotland

22 **Who should you ask to be a referee for a job application?**
Select two options from below

   A A previous employer

   B A close personal friend

   C A relative or family member

   D A college tutor

23 **Which of these statements is correct?**

   A The HM Revenue and Customs self-assessment helpline
         can provide help and advice on filling out tax forms

   B You can only get help filling out tax forms by
         paying for the services of an accountant

24 **If an employee's work, punctuality or attendance does not improve,
after being given a warning, then their employer can give them
notice to leave their job. Is this statement true or false?**

   A True

   B False

PRACTICE TEST 3

1 **Why did the UK encourage immigration in the 1950s?**

    A Because of an agreement with other Commonwealth countries

    B To meet an EU directive on immigration

    C To offer safety to people escaping persecution

    D To resolve a shortage of labour in the UK

2 **Which of these statements is correct?**

    A It is illegal to be drunk in public

    B It is illegal to be drunk anywhere

3 **What work did migrant Irish labourers do in the UK during the Irish famine?**

    A Build canals and railways

    B Drive local buses

    C Teach in schools

    D Work in textile mills

4 **When is Hallowe'en celebrated?**

    A 1 March

    B 31 October

    C 1 November

    D 30 November

5 **What is the title of the King or Queen within the Church of England?**

    A Archbishop of Canterbury

    B Governor General

    C Head Priest

    D Supreme Governor

6   How many years must have passed before an individual's census form is viewable by the public?

   A   10 years

   B   100 years

   C   50 years

   D   An individual's census form is confidential and never viewable by the public

7   What does Christmas Day celebrate?

   A   The birth of Jesus Christ

   B   The death of Jesus Christ

   C   The miracles of Jesus Christ

   D   The resurrection of Jesus Christ

**8   What is the role of a Member of Parliament?
Select two options from below**

   A   Scrutinise and comment on what the government is doing

   B   Elect Members of the House of Lords

   C   Vote in the European Parliament

   D   Represent their constituency

9   Non-departmental public bodies are under the political control of the government. Is this statement true or false?

   A   True

   B   False

10   Which of the following is not an agreement produced by the UN?

   A   The Convention on the Elimination of All Forms of Discrimination against Women

   B   The Convention on the Protection of the Ozone Layer

   C   The UN Convention on the Rights of the Child

   D   The Universal Declaration of Human Rights

11 How is it decided which party forms the Government?

    A The members of the House of Lords vote for their preferred party

    B The party that wins the majority of constituencies forms the Government

    C The party with the most candidates forms the Government

    D The party with the most votes forms the Government

12 To become a local councillor, a candidate must have a local connection with the area. Is this statement true or false?

    A True

    B False

13 The House of Commons can not overrule the decisions of the House of Lords. Is this statement true or false?

    A True

    B False

14 What are functions of the House of Lords? Select two options from below

    A Suggest amendments to laws

    B Propose new laws

    C Elect the Prime Minister

    D Elect the Speaker of the House of Commons

15 What is housing provided by local authorities often called?

    A Council housing

    B Free housing

    C Local housing

    D Market housing

16 **If you do not pay your electricity bill and the supply is cut off, you can be reconnected for free. Is this statement true or false?**

    A True

    B False ✓

17 **Which of these statements is correct?**

    A If you lose your cash or debit card you must inform the bank immediately ✓

    B If you lose your cash or debit card you should only inform the bank if you are sure it has been stolen

18 **What does NHS stand for?**

    A National Health Service ✓

    B National Hockey Stadium

    C National Horse Show

    D New Homes Show

19 **What is the speed limit on single carriageways?**

    A 60 miles per hour ✓

    B 70 miles per hour

    C 80 miles per hour

    D 90 miles per hour

20 **When you stay overnight in hospital you need to provide your own meals. Is this statement true or false?**

    A True ✓

    B False ✗

21 **Which of these statements is correct?**

    A Schools can choose to provide religious education to pupils ✓

    B Parents are allowed to withdraw their children from religious education lessons ✗

22 When looking for employment, what is the purpose of a referee?

 A To negotiate pay after a successful interview

 B To resolve any disputes between you and your employer

 C To search for jobs that match your skills

 D To write a report about a person's suitability for a job

23 What are National Insurance contributions used for?
Select two options from below

 A To contribute to your State Retirement Pension

 B To help fund the National Health Service

 C To pay for education and community services

 D To pay for police and armed services

24 When might you be entitled to redundancy pay?
Select two options from below

 A The job is no longer needed by the employer

 B The employer can not afford to pay for the job

 C If you are dismissed from your job

 D If you meet performance targets set by your employer

PRACTICE TEST 4

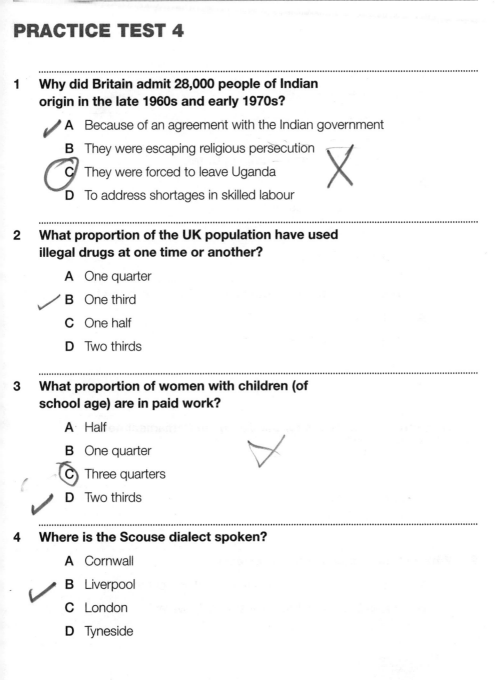

1   Why did Britain admit 28,000 people of Indian origin in the late 1960s and early 1970s?

A   Because of an agreement with the Indian government

B   They were escaping religious persecution

C   They were forced to leave Uganda

D   To address shortages in skilled labour

2   What proportion of the UK population have used illegal drugs at one time or another?

A   One quarter

B   One third

C   One half

D   Two thirds

3   What proportion of women with children (of school age) are in paid work?

A   Half

B   One quarter

C   Three quarters

D   Two thirds

4   Where is the Scouse dialect spoken?

A   Cornwall

B   Liverpool

C   London

D   Tyneside

5   When is Guy Fawkes Night?

   A   The evening of 15 October

   B   The evening of 25 September

   C   The evening of 30 May

   D   The evening of 5 November ✓

6   What is the largest ethnic minority in Britain?

   A   Bangladeshi descent

   B   Black Caribbean descent

   C   Indian descent ✓

   D   Pakistani descent

7   What percentage of the UK's ethnic minorities live in the London area?

   A   14%

   B   30%

   C   45% ✓

   D   60%

8   How often are elections for the European Parliament held?

   A   Every year

   B   Every four years

   C   Every five years ✓

   D   Every ten years

9   Which of these statements is correct?

   A   Proceedings in Parliament are never made public

   B   Proceedings in Parliament are publicly available ✓

10 **The UK is a member of the European Union but not of the Council of Europe. Is this statement true or false?**

A True

(B) False

11 **How often does the Cabinet normally meet?**

A Bi-weekly

B Daily

C Monthly

D Weekly

12 **What is the name of the official record of proceedings in Parliament?**

(A) Hansard

B Parliament News

C The Recorder

D Westminster Hour

13 **How many constituencies are there throughout the United Kingdom?**

A 1,105

B 350

C 646

D 750

14 **What are two key features of the civil service? Select two options from below**

A Political neutrality

B Professionalism

C Business knowledge

D Party loyalty

15 Which of the following statements is correct?

    A Everyone is entitled to apply for council accommodation

    B Only people on benefits are entitled to apply for council accommodation

16 Who is responsible for the collection of refuse?

    A The local authority

    B The NHS

    C The police

    D Your landlord

17 Select the correct statement from below

    A Children aged 14 to 16 can be employed to do any form of work as long as they are properly trained

    B It is illegal to employ children aged 14 to 16 to do work that might cause them any kind of injury

18 Which of these statements is correct?

    A General Practitioners always work together in group practices

    B Group practices of General Practitioners are sometimes called Primary Health Care Centres

19 Who is responsible for organising the health treatment you receive?

    A A specialist

    B The local authority

    C Your GP

    D Your local MP

20 Which of these statements is correct?

    A Some dentists have two sets of charges, both NHS and private

    B All dentists work for the NHS

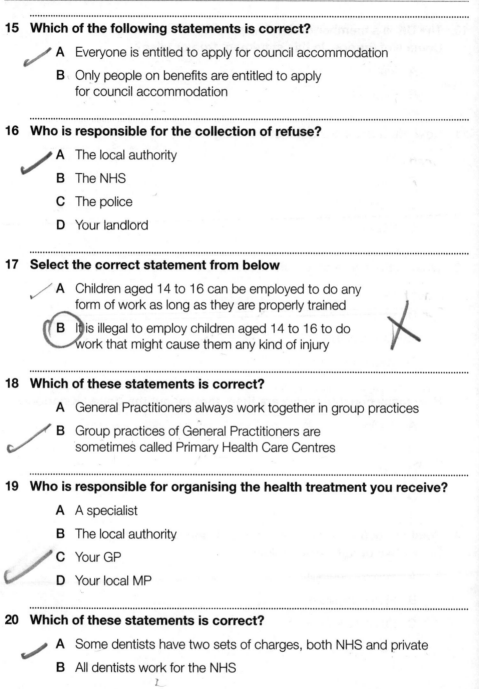

21   At what ages are Key Stage Tests held in England?

   A   10, 12 and 14

   B   11, 15 and 17

   C   7 and 15

   D   7, 11 and 14

22   When might you need a CRB check?

   A   When applying for welfare benefits

   B   When applying for work that involves children or vulnerable people

   C   When buying a house

   D   When requesting medical treatment from the NHS

23   What happens if you do not pay enough NI contributions?
Select two options from below

   A   You will not be entitled to certain benefits such as
       Jobseeker's Allowance or Maternity Pay

   B   You may not receive a full state retirement pension

   C   You will be fined and need to sign up to a repayment plan

   D   You will be prosecuted and may face a prison sentence

24   Between what ages can men claim the Jobseeker's Allowance?

   A   16–65 years old

   B   18–60 years old

   C   18–65 years old

   D   21–65 years old

PRACTICE TEST 5

1   Select the correct statement

    A   Children are free to work at any time of the day

    ✓**B**   It is illegal for a child to work before 7am or after 7pm

2   What proportion of young adults in the UK have used illegal drugs at one time or another?

    A   One quarter

    ✓**B**   One third

    C   One half

    D   Two thirds

3   Very few people believe that women in Britain should stay at home and not go out to paid work. Is this statement true or false?

    A   True

    ✓**B**   False

4   What is a census?

    A   A count of the whole population

    B   A form required for postal voting

    C   A traditional English festival

    ✓**D**   The government department that collects statistics

5   What traditionally happens on April Fool's Day?

    A   It is a public holiday until noon

    B   People enjoy public fireworks displays

    ✓**C**   People play jokes on each other

    D   None of the above

6 **Where is the Welsh language widely spoken?**

    A Highlands and Islands of Scotland

    B Ireland

    C Southern England

    D Wales ✓

7 **Britain has an ageing population and has a record number of people aged 85 and over. Is this statement true or false?**

    A True ✓

    B False

8 **The 'first past the post' system is used to elect Members of the European Parliament. Is this statement true or false?**

    A True ✓

    B False

9 **Newspaper owners and editors do not try to influence public opinion. Is this statement true or false?**

    A True

    B False ✓

10 **What type of constitution does the UK have?**

    A A legal constitution ✓

    B A written constitution

    C An amended constitution

    D An unwritten constitution

11 **Members of the public are not able to visit the Houses of Parliament. Is this statement true or false?**

    A True ✓

    B False

12 Which politicians are members of the Shadow Cabinet?

    A Civil servants working for the government

    B Peers from the House of Lords

    C Senior members of the main opposition party

    D The remaining MPs in Government who are not in the Cabinet

13 What is a Civil Servant?

    A A manager or administrator who carries out government policy

    B A manager or administrator who works for the House of Lords

    C A member of a political party

    D A Member of Parliament

14 What is an important ceremonial role that the King or Queen performs?

    A Chairing proceedings in the House of Lords

    B Meeting weekly with the Prime Minister

    C Opening of a new parliamentary session

    D Voting in the House of Commons

15 In many areas of the UK there is a shortage of council accommodation. Is this statement true or false?

    A True

    B False

16 How are local government services paid for?
Select two options from below

    A Grants from central government

    B Council tax

    C Charitable donations

    D Insurance premiums

17 What will happen if you do not pay the total amount of your monthly credit card bill?

    A Nothing

    B You will be charged interest

    C You will be required to return the card to the credit card company

    D You will be unable to use the card until the bill is paid

18 Which of these statements is correct?

    A Tickets for trains are usually bought before you get on the train

    B Tickets for trains are usually bought when you have reached your destination

19 Which of these statements is correct?

    A In an emergency you can attend a hospital, but only if you have a letter from your GP

    B In an emergency you should go to the Accident and Emergency department of your nearest hospital

20 Which of these statements is correct?

    A You can get regular ante-natal care from your local hospital, local health centre or from special ante-natal clinics

    B Ante-natal care is only available from special private clinics and is not part of the NHS

21 If your child's main language is not English they can get extra support from a specialist teacher. What is this teacher called?

    A EAL teacher

    B PAL teacher

    C LLL teacher

    D ESE teacher

22 **It is compulsory for employees to join a trade union.**
Is this statement true or false?

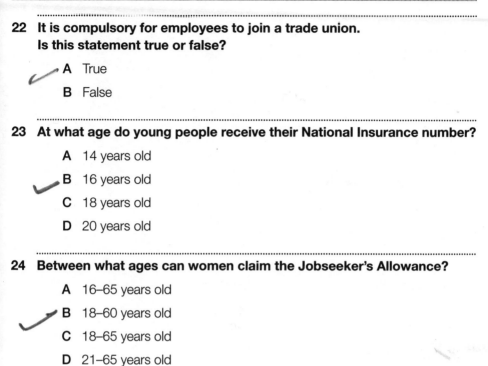

    A True

    B False

23 **At what age do young people receive their National Insurance number?**

    A 14 years old

    B 16 years old

    C 18 years old

    D 20 years old

24 **Between what ages can women claim the Jobseeker's Allowance?**

    A 16–65 years old

    B 18–60 years old

    C 18–65 years old

    D 21–65 years old

PRACTICE TEST 6

1   Why were recruitment centres set up in the West Indies in the 1950s?

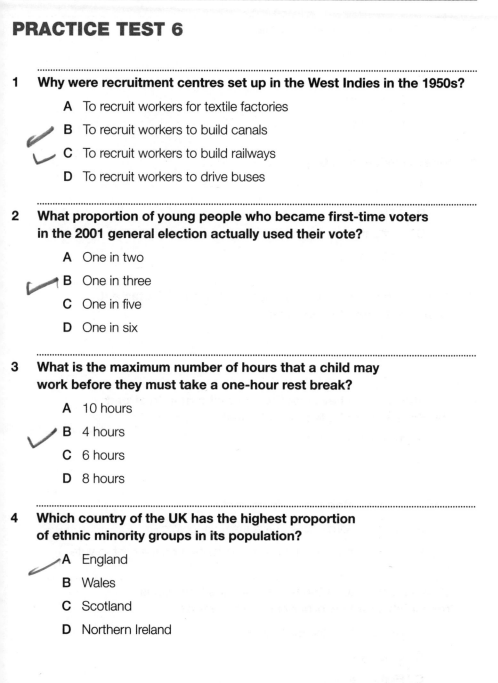

A   To recruit workers for textile factories

B   To recruit workers to build canals

C   To recruit workers to build railways

D   To recruit workers to drive buses

2   What proportion of young people who became first-time voters in the 2001 general election actually used their vote?

A   One in two

B   One in three

C   One in five

D   One in six

3   What is the maximum number of hours that a child may work before they must take a one-hour rest break?

A   10 hours

B   4 hours

C   6 hours

D   8 hours

4   Which country of the UK has the highest proportion of ethnic minority groups in its population?

A   England

B   Wales

C   Scotland

D   Northern Ireland

5   What is the population of England?

    A 23.4 million

    B 38.1 million

    C 50.1 million

    D 58.8 million ✓

6   When is Valentine's Day?

    A 1 April

    B 1 February

    C 14 April

    D 14 February ✓

7   The Queen must not marry anyone who is not Protestant. Is this statement true or false?

    A True ✓

    B False

8   Hereditary peers have lost the automatic right to attend the House of Lords. Is this statement true or false?

    A True

    B False ✓

9   Which of these statements is correct?

    A Only UK born citizens have the right to vote

    B Both UK born and naturalised citizens have the right to vote ✓

10   What is the name of the ministerial position that is responsible for law, order and immigration?

    A Chancellor of the Exchequer ✓

    B Chief Whip

    C Home Secretary

    D Lord Chancellor

11 **Who is the current heir to the throne?**

    A Prince William

    B The Duke of Edinburgh

    C The Duke of York

    D The Prince of Wales

12 **The Government has the power to instruct the police to follow its instructions on what to do in a particular case.**
Is this statement true or false?

    A True

    B False

13 **The Council of Europe has no power to make laws.**
Is this statement true or false?

    A True

    B False

14 **Which of the following statements is correct about political reporting during election periods in the UK? Select two options from below**

    A Television channels have to give equal time to rival viewpoints

    B All reporting on radio and television must be balanced

    C It is illegal for newspapers to run campaigns to influence people's opinions

    D Politicians must be able to read interview questions beforehand

15 **Housing associations are run by the government.**
Is this statement true or false?

    A True

    B False

16 **If only one person lives in a house how much reduction do they get on their Council Tax?**

    A 5%

    B 25%

    C 50%

    D 75%

17 **What is the role of the National Trust?**

    A Collect the TV licence

    B Guarantee a pension for government employees

    C Maintain and enhance the residence of the Prime Minister

    D Preserve important buildings and countryside in the UK

18 **All taxis and minicabs must be licensed and display a licence plate. Is this statement true or false?**

    A True

    B False

19 **When should you look for a GP?**

    A As soon as you move to a new area

    B Once you have registered with the local authority

    C When you become ill

    D When you visit the local hospital

20 **Who provides regular contact and advice to parents after a child is born and up until it is five years old?**

    A A health visitor

    B A midwife

    C A specialist

    D An optician

21 **In England careers advice for children 14 and over is available from Connexions. Is this statement true or false?**

   A True

   B False

22 **Select the correct statement**

   A It is illegal to discriminate against someone for employment in any circumstances

   B Discrimination is not against the law when the job involves working for someone in their own home

23 **At what age can men get a state pension?**

   A 55 years old

   B 60 years old

   C 65 years old

   D 70 years old

24 **Select the correct statement**

   A You must be at least 18 years old to be eligible for a Young Person's Bridging Allowance

   B You must be 16 or 17 years old to be eligible for a Young Person's Bridging Allowance

PRACTICE TEST 7

1 **In the early 1990s, groups of people from the former Soviet Union came to Britain looking for a new and safer way of life. Is this statement true or false?**

    A True

    B False

2 **How long was Britain at war during the Second World War?**

    A 2 years

    B 4 years

    C 6 years

    D 8 years

3 **What percentage of the workforce are women?**

    A 40%

    B 45%

    C 51%

    D 65%

4 **When is Boxing Day?**

    A 1 January

    B 25 December

    C 26 December

    D 31 December

5 **Which other name can be used to refer to the Church of England?**

    A The Anglican Church

    B The Catholic Church

    C The Methodist Church

    D The Presbyterian Church

6   What sport is played at the Wimbledon tournament?

    A Cricket

    B Football

    C Rugby

    D Tennis

7   What percentage of Christians in the UK are Roman Catholic?

    A 10%

    B 20%

    C 30%

    D 40%

8   What is the name of the country house of the Prime Minister?

    A 10 Downing Street

    B Balmoral Castle

    C Chequers

    D Palace of Westminster

9   Which of the following statements is correct?

    A Citizens of EU states who are resident in the UK can not vote in national parliamentary elections

    B Citizens of EU states who are resident in the UK can vote in all public elections

10   A Prime Minister can be removed from office by their party at any time. Is this statement true or false?

    A True

    B False

11 **Where do local authorities get most of their funding from?**

   A Government taxation

   B Issuing parking tickets

   C Local council tax

   D Lottery grants

12 **Who is the Head of State of the United Kingdom?**

   A The Home Secretary

   B The King or Queen

   C The Prime Minister

   D The Speaker of the House of Commons

13 **When was the Council of Europe established?**

   A 1901

   B 1949

   C 1964

   D 1982

14 **What are important roles of the Prime Minister?**
   Select two options from below

   A Appoint the members of the Cabinet

   B Leader of the party in power

   C Perform the duties of Head of State

   D Effect new laws by giving royal assent to legislation

15 **What is contained in an inventory, when one is attached to a tenancy agreement?**

   A A list of all furniture and fittings in a property

   B A list of all people who have lived in a property

   C A record of the rent paid for a property

   D Information about the owner of a property

16 **If you buy a home with a mortgage, you must insure the building against fire, theft and accidental damage.**
Is this statement true or false?

    A True

    B False

17 **People borrowing money from banks to pay for cars and holidays is more common in the UK than in many other countries.**
Is this statement true or false?

    A True

    B False

18 **What is the minimum age required to drive a car?**

    A 16 years old

    B 17 years old

    C 18 years old

    D 21 years old

19 **Which of these statements is correct?**

    A An identity card is the only document that can be used to prove your identity

    B A driving licence or a recent phone bill may be used to prove your identity

20 **What does the Family Planning Association provide advice on?**
Select two options from below

    A Sexual heath

    B Contraception

    C Family values

    D Ambulance services

21 **Parents are not allowed to sit on a school's governing body.**
Is this statement true or false?

    A True

    B False

22 **By law, men and women who do the same job should**
receive equal pay. Is this statement true or false?

    A True

    B False

23 **At what age can women get a state pension?**

    A 55 years old

    B 60 years old

    C 65 years old

    D 70 years old

24 **Which of the following statements is correct?**

    A As soon as you become self-employed you should register yourself for National Insurance and tax by contacting HM Revenue and Customs

    B It is not necessary to contact the HM Revenue and Customs when you become self-employed

PRACTICE TEST 8

1   **What is the purpose of the Council of Europe?**

    A   To create a single market for members of the council

    B   To create new European regulations and directives

    C   To debate proposals, decisions and expenditure
       of the European Commission

    D   To develop conventions which focus on human rights,
       democracy, education, the environment, health and culture

2   **Why did large numbers of Jewish people
come to Britain during 1880–1910?**

    A   To escape famine

    B   To escape racist attacks

    C   To invade and seize land

    D   To work in textile factories

3   **When did the First World War end?**

    A   1914

    B   1918

    C   1925

    D   1945

4   **Which of these statements is correct?**

    A   Boxing Day and New Year are both public holidays

    B   New Year is a public holiday and Boxing Day is not

5 **Where is the Cockney dialect spoken?**

    A Cornwall

    B Liverpool

    C London

    D Tyneside

6 **Why was a census not carried out in the United Kingdom in 1941?**

    A Because Britain was at war

    B Because it was abolished by the government

    C Because it was boycotted by the public

    D No census was planned for that year

7 **The employment of children in the UK is strictly controlled by law. Is this statement true or false?**

    A True

    B False

8 **What is the name of the ministerial position that is responsible for legal affairs?**

    A Chancellor of the Exchequer

    B Foreign Secretary

    C Home Secretary

    D Lord Chancellor

9 **In which elections can European citizens vote? Select two answers from below**

    A European elections

    B Local elections

    C National elections

    D Elections to the House of Lords

10 Which one of the following parliaments or assemblies does not use proportional representation?

    A House of Commons

    B Northern Ireland Assembly

    C Welsh Assembly

    D Scottish Parliament

11 What is the role of the Cabinet?

    A To examine laws proposed by the House of Commons

    B To investigate serious complaints against the police

    C To make decisions about government policy

    D To provide royal assent for new laws

12 Which of the following are not mandatory services provided by local authorities?

    A Education

    B Fire service

    C Refuse collection

    D None – they are all mandatory services provided by local authorities

13 What is the United Kingdom's role with in the United Nations?

    A Member of the UN Security Council

    B Provides a neutral location for hosting UN meetings in Scotland

    C Selects the UN Secretary General from members of the Security Council

    D All of the above

14 Which of these statements is correct?

    A The House of Commons is the more important of the two chambers in Parliament

    B The House of Lords is the more important of the two chambers in Parliament

15 Which statement is correct?

    A When you rent a home privately you sign
a tenancy agreement or lease

    B When you agree to buy a home you sign
a tenancy agreement or lease

**16 Who should you speak to if you have trouble with your neighbours?
Select two options from below**

    A Your landlord

    B The local authority

    C The bank

    D Your GP

17 Which of these statements is correct?

    A If you are refused a loan you have the right to ask the reason why

    B Banks only take your previous credit record into
account when making a decision about a loan

**18 What is the maximum number of hours that a child
can work on a school day or Sunday?**

    A Eight hours

    B Four hours

    C Six hours

    D Two hours

19 At what age do children in England go to secondary school?

    A 11

    B 12

    C 15

    D 9

20 Within what period of time must a baby be registered with the Registrar of Births, Marriages and Deaths?

    A One week

    B Six months

    C Six weeks

    D Twelve months

21 How many days a year must a school open?

    A 100 days

    B 150 days

    C 190 days

    D 365 days

22 It is illegal for a child to work for more than one hour before school starts. Is this statement true or false?

    A True

    B False

23 Where can you apply for a National Insurance number? Select two options from below

    A Any Jobcentre Plus branch

    B Your local Social Security Office

    C Your local library

    D Your local council or town hall

24 British citizens require a work permit before they can work in any country that is a member of the European Economic Area. Is this statement true or false?

    A True

    B False

PRACTICE TEST 9

1   Which of these statements is correct?

    A In 19th century Britain, women had fewer rights than men

    B Women have always had the same rights as men

2   When were women over 30 given the right to vote?

    A 1840

    B 1901

    C 1918

    D 1945

3   How often do most children in the UK receive their pocket money?

    A Every day

    B Every month

    C Every week

    D Only on their birthday

4   What is the Grand National?

    A A tennis tournament

    B A football cup

    C A golf championship

    D A horse race

5   What does Remembrance Day commemorate?

    A The appreciation of single mothers

    B The celebration of community

    C The crucifixion of Jesus Christ

    D The memory of those who died fighting in wars

6   What percentage of the UK population is made up of ethnic minorities?

    A About 15%

    B About 2%

    C About 25%

    D About 8%

7   What do people sometimes do on Valentine's Day?

    A Fast from eating for the whole day

    B Play jokes on each other until midday

    C Send anonymous cards to someone they secretly admire

    D Wear poppies in memory of St Valentine

8   Which minister can sit in the House of Lords or in the House of Commons?

    A Chancellor of the Exchequer

    B Foreign Secretary

    C Lord Chancellor

    D Home Secretary

9   How often is the electoral register updated?

    A Every five years

    B Every time somebody moves house

    C Every two years

    D Every year

10   When are local government elections held?

    A April every two years

    B June and December each year

    C May each year

    D September each year

11 How many politicians are there in the Cabinet?

    A About 10

    B About 20

    C About 30

    D About 40

12 Which of these statements is correct?

    A The Metropolitan Police is based at New Scotland Yard

    B The Metropolitan Police is based in the Palace of Westminster

13 How is the Speaker of the House of Commons chosen?

    A Appointed by the King or Queen

    B Chosen by the Prime Minister

    C Elected by fellow MPs

    D Elected by the public

14 When is a jury used?

    A To choose an appropriate penalty for someone found guilty of a serious crime

    B To confirm decisions made by a judge

    C To decide if someone is innocent or guilty of a serious crime

    D To decide if someone is innocent or guilty of a less important crime

15 Why will you be asked to give a landlord a deposit at the beginning of your tenancy?

    A To cover the cost of any damage to the property

    B To pay for electricity supply at the property

    C To pay for keys to the property

    D To start a bank account

16   What does the film classification U means?

A   Children under 15 are not allowed to see or rent the film

B   No one under 18 is allowed to see or rent the film

C   Suitable for anyone aged four years or over

D   Suitable for everyone but some parts of the
film might be unsuitable for children

17   What is the minimum age to be able to drink alcohol in a pub?

A   16 years old

B   18 years old

C   21 years old

D   It depends if you are with an adult

**18   From where did the government encourage immigrant workers
to help British reconstruction after the Second World War?**

A   Ireland, other parts of Europe and the West Indies

B   America and other parts of North America

C   Australia and other parts of Oceania

D   India, Pakistan and Bangladesh

**19   You can not be arrested if you refuse to take a breathalyser test.
Is this statement true or false?**

A   True

B   False

**20   Education in the UK is free and voluntary for children between
the ages of 5 and 16. Is this statement true or false?**

A   True

B   False

21 **What is the financial help called that is available to young people from low income families who leave school early?**

    A After School Allowance

    B Education Maintenance Allowance

    C Housing Benefit

    D School Leaver's Payment

22 **In Northern Ireland, it is legal to discriminate on grounds of religious belief or political opinion. Is this statement true or false?**

    A True

    B False

23 **For what reason could you be immediately dismissed from your job?**

    A Because of serious misconduct

    B Because of your age

    C Because of your religious beliefs

    D Because of your sexuality

24 **What is the minimum number of weeks maternity leave that women are entitled to?**

    A 11 weeks

    B 16 weeks

    C 21 weeks

    D 26 weeks

PRACTICE TEST 10

1   Which of these statements is correct?

   A   In the 1960s and 1970s Parliament passed laws
   giving women the right to equal pay

   B   In the 1960s and 1970s Parliament passed laws allowing employers
   to discriminate against women because of their gender

**2   Cigarette consumption by adults in Britain has risen significantly.
Is this statement true or false?**

   A   True

   B   False

**3   During the 1980s, the largest immigrant groups
to the UK came from which countries?**

   A   China, Japan and South Korea

   B   India, Pakistan, Sri Lanka and Bangladesh

   C   Russia, Poland, Belarus and Ukraine

   D   United States, Australia, South Africa and New Zealand

4   How might you stop young people playing tricks on you at Hallowe'en?

   A   Call the police

   B   Give them some money

   C   Give them sweets or chocolates

   D   Hide from them

5   What does the abbreviation FA stand for?

   A   A Federal Agent

   B   The Fine Arts

   C   The Football Association

   D   The Fourth Amendment

6   What percentage of the UK population say they attend religious services?

   A   Around 10%

   B   Around 20%

   C   Around 30%

   D   Around 40%

7   What traditionally happens on Mother's Day?

   A   Mothers make special meals for their families

   B   People celebrate the mother of Jesus Christ

   C   People give cards or gifts to their mothers

   D   People hold fireworks displays

8   Someone is more likely to be elected as an MP if they have been nominated to represent a major political party. Is this statement true or false?

   A   True

   B   False

9   It is not possible to see the electoral register as this would damage the privacy of voters. Is this statement true or false?

   A   True

   B   False

10   Britain was a founding member of the EU. Is this statement true or false?

   A   True

   B   False

11 Which of the following parliaments or assemblies use proportional representation?

A Scottish Parliament

B Northern Ireland Assembly

C European Parliament

D All of the above

12 What is the purpose of the United Nations?

A To create a single market for all world nations

B To create global laws to regulate foreign affairs

C To debate global third world development and funding proposals

D To prevent war and promote international peace and security

13 What is the name of the system that governs how MPs are elected into the House of Commons?

A Aggregated vote system

B Electoral college system

C First past the post system

D Proportional representation system

14 Who is the head of the Commonwealth?

A The Archbishop of Canterbury

B The British Prime Minister

C The Queen

D The Secretary of the Commonwealth

15 A deposit paid to the landlord at the beginning of a tenancy is usually equal to one month's rent. Is this statement true or false?

A True

B False

16 What does the film classification PG mean?

  A Children under 15 are not allowed to see or rent the film

  B No one under 18 is allowed to see or rent the film

  C Suitable for anyone aged four years or over

  D Suitable for everyone but some parts of the
        film might be unsuitable for children

**17 Interest rates in credit unions are usually higher than banks.
    Is this statement true or false?**

  A True

  B False

18 Select the correct statement

  A Children are allowed to work for the full
        duration of their school holidays

  B Children must have at least two consecutive weeks a
        year during their holidays where they do not work

19 If you cannot find a GP, who can you ask for help to find one?

  A Citizens Advice Bureau

  B The local health authority

  C The local hospital

  D Your local MP

**20 If a child does not attend school, that child's parent or guardian
    may be prosecuted. Is this statement true or false?**

  A True

  B False

21 **What are courses for people who want to improve their English language skills called?**

    A EAL

    B EEE

    C ESOL

    D NHS

22 **What types of discrimination can the Equal Opportunities Commission help with?**

    A Discrimination related to disability

    B Racial discrimination

    C Religious discrimination

    D Sex discrimination

23 **Select the correct statement**

    A Many people receive pensions through their work or pay into personal pension plans

    B People can only pay into and receive State Pensions

24 **Women are only entitled to maternity leave after they have completed their first year in a job. Is this statement true or false?**

    A True

    B False

PRACTICE TEST 11

1 **On average, boys leave school with better qualifications than girls. Is this statement true or false?**

    A True

    B False

2 **Why did Irish migrants come to Britain during the mid 1840s?**

    A To escape famine

    B To escape religious persecution

    C To invade and seize land

    D To seek refuge from war

3 **How many young people (up to the age of 19) are there in the UK?**

    A 10 million

    B 15 million

    C 20 million

    D 5 million

4 **How often is a census carried out in the United Kingdom?**

    A Once every eight years

    B Once every five years

    C Once every ten years

    D Whenever the government decides

5 **When was the first census carried out in the United Kingdom?**

    A 1785

    B 1801

    C 1851

    D 1912

6 Where is the Gaelic language spoken?

    A Cornwall

    B Scotland and Northern Ireland

    C Southern England

    D Wales

7 What is the name of the patron saint of Wales?

    A St Andrew

    B St David

    C St George

    D St Patrick

8 In England, when do most young people take GCSE examinations?

    A 15 years old

    B 16 years old

    C 17 years old

    D 18 years old

9 What may prevent you from being able to stand for public office? Select two options from below

    A Being a member of the armed forces

    B Having been found guilty of a criminal offence

    C Being a Commonwealth citizen

    D Being a citizen of the Irish Republic

10 Which of these statements is correct?

    A Subject to some restrictions, citizens of the European Union have the right to work in any EU member state

    B Citizens of the European Union must have a valid work permit to work in any EU member state

11 In which year did Queen Elizabeth II start her reign?

    A 1945

    B 1952

    C 1963

    D 1972

12 How do you register to vote?

    A Bring your passport to any polling booth on election day

    B Contact your local council election registration office

    C Contact your local MP's office

    D Do nothing – all eligible citizens are automatically registered

13 All candidates standing for office in local government must be members of a political party. Is this statement true or false?

    A True

    B False

14 If you are the tenant of a property then you do not have to pay Council Tax. Is this statement true or false?

    A True

    B False

15 What do children aged 14 to 16 need from their local authority if they want to work? Select two options from below

    A An employment card

    B Proof of identity

    C Certificate of fitness for work

    D A National Insurance number

16 **What denomination of bank notes do not exist in the UK?**

    A £5

    B £20

    C £50

    D £500

17 **People under 18 cannot drink alcohol in a pub but they can buy it in a supermarket or an off-licence. Is this statement true or false?**

    A True

    B False

18 **Which of these statements is correct?**

    A A judge can only decide on the penalty for a person found guilty of a serious crime

    B A judge can decide whether a person is guilty or innocent of a serious crime

19 **What is the role of the European Commission?**
Select two options from below

    A Draft proposals for new EU policies and laws

    B Administer EU funding programmes

    C Select the members of the European Parliament

    D Select the members of the Council of Ministers

20 **At what age can children in the UK choose to leave school?**

    A 12

    B 14

    C 16

    D 18

21 **University students in England, Wales and Northern Ireland do not have to pay tuition fees. Is this statement true or false?**

    A True

    B False

22 **A written contract for employment is very useful if there is ever a disagreement about your work, pay or conditions. Is this statement true or false?**

    A True

    B False

23 **What is the purpose of a National Insurance number?**

    A To allow companies to check your credit history

    B To prove that you have British nationality

    C To prove that you have adequate home insurance

    D To track National Insurance contributions

24 **Select the correct statement**

    A Only women that have full-time employment are entitled to maternity leave

    B Maternity leave rights apply to both full-time and part-time workers

PRACTICE TEST 12

1   Who were Suffragettes?

    A Nurses that cared for the elderly

    B Representatives of people seeking asylum

    C Refugee care workers

    D Campaigners for greater rights for women

2   What year did women in the UK gain the right to divorce their husband?

    A 1810

    B 1857

    C 1901

    D 1945

3   When you make an offer on a home you want to buy, why must the offer be 'subject to contract'?

    A So that you can withdraw if there are reasons you cannot complete the purchase

    B So the local authority can review the offer

    C So the purchase can be completed as quickly as possible

    D So the seller can check if they can get a better offer elsewhere

4   What was the population of the United Kingdom in 2005?

    A 39.3 million

    B 49.8 million

    C 59.8 million

    D 98.3 million

5 When did the Church of England come in to existence?

    A In the 1440s

    B In the 1530s

    C In the 1640s

    D In the 1750s

6 What is traditionally eaten on Christmas Day?

    A Beer-battered cod and chips

    B Poached salmon

    C Roast pork and trifle

    D Turkey

7 What overall proportion of Britain's African Caribbean, Pakistani, Indian and Bangladeshi communities were born in Britain?

    A About half

    B About one quarter

    C About one third

    D About three quarters

8 Which voting system is used to elect the Scottish Parliament and the Welsh Assembly?

    A A ranking or preferential system

    B Assembly members are chosen by the government

    C 'First past the post'

    D Proportional representation

9 Members of the House of Lords can stand for election to the House of Commons. Is this statement true or false?

    A True

    B False

10 What is the current voting age?

    A 16 years old

    B 18 years old

    C 20 years old

    D 21 years old

11 When did the government start a programme of devolved administration for Wales and Scotland?

    A 1979

    B 1982

    C 1997

    D 2001

12 Where is the Prime Minister's official residence?

    A 10 Downing Street

    B 12 Downing Street

    C Buckingham Palace

    D Palace of Westminster

13 Which country does not have its own parliament or national assembly?

    A England

    B Northern Ireland

    C Scotland

    D Wales

14 What proportion of people in the UK own their own home?

    A Half

    B One-quarter

    C One-third

    D Two-thirds

15 A tenancy agreement will be for a fixed period of time. Is this statement true or false?

   A   True

   B   False

16 Bank notes from Scotland and Northern Ireland are not valid in the rest of the UK. Is this statement true or false?

   A   True

   B   False

17 Insurance for a car or motorcycle is optional. Is this statement true or false?

   A   True

   B   False

18 At what voltage is electricity supplied in the UK?

   A   1000 volts

   B   110 volts

   C   240 volts

   D   50 volts

19 When are you likely to be required to prove your identity? Select two options from below

   A   When opening a bank account

   B   When applying for Housing Benefit

   C   When purchasing National Rail tickets

   D   When travelling between England and Wales

20 In primary schools boys and girls usually learn together. Is this statement true or false?

   A   True

   B   False

21 What is the purpose of Housing Benefit?

    A To help you buy a home

    B To help you fix a home

    C To help you pay your rent

    D To help you sell a home

22 What is the minimum wage for workers aged 22 and above?

    A £3.30 an hour

    B £4.45 an hour

    C £5.35 an hour

    D £6.15 an hour

23 Select the correct statement

    A Refugees that have had successful asylum applications can only work in specific areas

    B Refugees that have had successful asylum applications have the same rights to work as UK citizens

24 All women workers are entitled to maternity pay. Is this statement true or false?

    A True

    B False

PRACTICE TEST 13

1 **Despite existing laws, women still do not always have the same access to promotion and better paid jobs as men.**
Is this statement true or false?

    A True

    B False

2 **What is the minimum age for buying tobacco?**

    A 14 years old

    B 16 years old

    C 18 years old

    D 21 years old

3 **Why did Protestant Huguenots from France come to Britain?**

    A To escape famine

    B To escape religious persecution

    C To invade and seize land

    D To seek refuge from war

4 **According to the 2001 Census, what percentage of the UK population reported that they had a religion?**

    A 35%

    B 55%

    C 65%

    D 75%

5 **What do people wear on Remembrance Day in memory of those who have died at war?**

    A Black clothing

    B Military clothing

    C Poppies

    D Red ribbons

6 **What is the name of the patron saint of England?**

    A St Andrew

    B St David

    C St George

    D St Patrick

7 **What percentage of London's population is made up of ethnic minorities?**

    A 15% of London's population

    B 29% of London's population

    C 45% of London's population

    D 9% of London's population

8 **Which policy areas have not been transferred to the Welsh Assembly or the Scottish Parliament and remain under central UK government control? Select two options from below**

    A Defence

    B Foreign affairs

    C Education

    D Health

9   Which of the following statements regarding the Commonwealth is not correct?

   A   It aims to promote democracy

   B   It can suspend the membership of a country

   C   It has no power over its members

   D   Membership is compulsory

10   What is the second largest party in the House of Commons called?

   A   Shadow Cabinet

   B   The Conservation Party

   C   The Labour Party

   D   The Opposition

11   Most of the countries that are members of the Commonwealth were part of the British Empire. Is this statement true or false?

   A   True

   B   False

12   What is the abbreviation MP short for?

   A   Master of Parliament

   B   Member of Parliament

   C   Member of Party

   D   Minister of Parliament

13   If you feel you have been unfairly dismissed from your job, what is the normal time period in which you can make a complaint to an Employment Tribunal?

   A   Two weeks

   B   Three weeks

   C   Two months

   D   Three months

14 People in the UK who buy their own home usually pay for it with a mortgage. Is this statement true or false?

    A True

    B False

15 A tenant must leave a home if the landlord has a court order requiring the tenant to do so. Is this statement true or false?

    A True

    B False

16 When will the British government adopt the euro as the UK's currency?

    A 2010

    B 2015

    C Never

    D When the British people vote for it in a referendum

17 Somebody aged 16 can drink wine or beer with a meal in a hotel or restaurant. Is this statement true or false?

    A True

    B False

18 If you have a driving licence from a country outside the EU, you may use it in the UK for up to 12 months. Is this statement true or false?

    A True

    B False

19 How can you compare qualifications from another country with those in the UK?

    A By asking your neighbour

    B By contacting the National Academic Recognition Information Centre

    C By visiting your local library

    D By writing to potential employers

20 Who should you approach to get information about local secondary schools?

    A NHS Direct

    B The local education authority

    C Your local MP

    D Your nearest school

21 Which of the following statements is correct?

    A If you need to see a specialist for medical treatment then you must see your GP first

    B You should always go directly to a specialist if you believe you know the medical treatment you require

22 What is the minimum wage for workers aged 18–21?

    A £3.30 an hour

    B £4.45 an hour

    C £5.35 an hour

    D £6.15 an hour

23 Select the correct statement

    A It is illegal to pay workers below the minimum wage

    B It is legal to pay workers below the minimum wage as long as they agree to the wage rate

24 Select the correct statement

    A Men are always entitled to paternity leave

    B Men must have worked for their employer at least 26 weeks before they are entitled to paternity leave

PRACTICE TEST 14

1   What percentage of children live in lone-parent families?

A   10%

B   25%

C   40%

D   55%

2   Name three countries that Jewish people migrated from (and into the UK) to escape persecution during 1880–1910

A   China, Japan, Korea

B   Israel, Egypt, Jordan

C   Poland, Ukraine, Belarus

D   USA, Canada, Mexico

3   What proportion of young people enrol to go on to higher education after school?

A   One in two

B   One in three

C   One in four

D   All young people move on to higher education

4   How is the Archbishop of Canterbury selected?

A   The monarch makes the selection based on the choice of the outgoing Archbishop of Canterbury

B   The monarch makes the selection based on the choice of the Prime Minister and a committee appointed by the Church of England

C   The selection is made by a vote in the House of Lords

D   The selection is made by public referendum

5   When is the national day for England?

   A   1 March

   B   17 March

   C   23 April

   D   30 November

6   How many bank holidays are there each year in the United Kingdom?

   A   Four

   B   Nine

   C   Ten

   D   Two

7   According to the 2001 Census, what percentage of people stated their religion as Muslim?

   A   Approximately 1%

   B   Approximately 15%

   C   Approximately 21%

   D   Approximately 3%

8   Can a judge change an Act of Parliament if it is incompatible with the Human Rights Act?

   A   Yes, but they must seek the Prime Minister's approval first

   B   Yes, but they must obtain permission from the Lord Chancellor

   C   Yes, but only if they believe the law is unfair

   D   No, but they can ask Parliament to consider doing so

9   How many countries are members of the European Union?

   A   12 countries

   B   15 countries

   C   27 countries

   D   41 countries

10 **How are Whips appointed?**

    A By the King or Queen

    B By the Prime Minister

    C By their party leaders

    D By vote amongst their peers

11 **What is a role of the European Parliament?**

    A Elect individual members of the European Commission

    B Ensure EU regulations and directives are being followed by member states

    C Examine decisions made by the European Council and the European Commission

    D Review European court cases that have been appealed

12 **The monarch rules the UK and can reject laws and decisions made by government and the Cabinet. Is this statement true or false?**

    A True

    B False

13 **What are functions of the Speaker of the House of Commons? Select two options from below**

    A To keep order during political debates

    B To make sure rules are followed in the House of Commons

    C To promote Members from the House of Commons to the House of Lords

    D To give royal assent to new laws agreed in the House of Commons

14 **Estate agents represent the person buying a house or flat. Is this statement true or false?**

    A True

    B False

15 Where should you go for help if you are homeless?

A To the local authority

B To the local hospital

C To your GP

D To your MP

16 Which of these statements is correct?

A No one younger than 18 may see an '18' rated film under any circumstances

B No one younger than 18 may see an '18' rated film unless they are with an adult

17 Foreign currency can only be bought or changed at post offices. Is this statement true or false?

A True

B False

18 Which of these statements is correct?

A It is a criminal offence to have a car without motor insurance

B It is not a criminal offence to have a car without motor insurance if you only drive it occasionally

19 Everything you tell your GP is confidential and cannot be passed on without your permission. Is this statement true or false?

A True

B False

20 **What information must an employer show on pay slips? Select two options from below**

    A Tax that has been deducted from your pay

    B National Insurance contributions that have been deducted from your pay

    C The number of days holiday entitlement that you have remaining

    D The date that your contract started

21 **Secondary schools are smaller than primary schools. Is this statement true or false?**

    A True

    B False

22 **What is the minimum wage for workers aged 16-17?**

    A £3.30 an hour

    B £4.45 an hour

    C £5.35 an hour

    D £6.15 an hour

23 **You can be dismissed for raising health and safety concerns. Is this statement true or false?**

    A True

    B False

24 **How many weeks of paid paternity leave are men entitled to?**

    A Four weeks

    B One week

    C Three weeks

    D Two weeks

PRACTICE TEST 15

1 **What percentage of children live within a stepfamily?**

    A 10%

    B 25%

    C 40%

    D 55%

2 **During the 1950s, where did Britain set up bus driver recruitment centres?**

    A Australia

    B Canada

    C Ireland

    D The West Indies

3 **How many children are estimated to be working in the United Kingdom?**

    A Eight million

    B Five million

    C One million

    D Two million

4 **When is New Year's Day?**

    A 1 January

    B 1 March

    C 25 December

    D 31 December

5   When is Remembrance Day?

    A 1 May

    B 11 November

    C 21 October

    D 31 August

6   Over the last 20 years, there has been a decline in population in the north east and north west of England. Is this statement true or false?

    A True

    B False

7   Where is the Geordie dialect spoken?

    A Cornwall

    B Liverpool

    C London

    D Tyneside

8   A judge can order a public body to change its practices or pay compensation if it is not respecting a person's human rights. Is this statement true or false?

    A True

    B False

9   Everyone in the UK has the legal right to practise the religion of their choice. Is this statement true or false?

    A True

    B False

10 What must a candidate achieve in order to win their constituency?

    A Be a member of the party that wins government office

    B Win at least 15,000 votes

    C Win at least 25% of the votes within their constituency

    D Win the most votes out of all candidates in their constituency

11 What is the current minimum age for standing for public office?

    A 18 years

    B 21 years

    C 25 years

    D 30 years

12 What is the name of the largest police force in the United Kingdom?

    A Humberside Police

    B Merseyside Police

    C The Bill

    D The Metropolitan Police

13 How is the NHS Direct service provided?

    A At your GP's surgery

    B At your nearest hospital

    C Over the telephone

    D Using a mobile surgery or ambulance

14 You can only find information about homes for sale in local newspapers. Is this statement true or false?

    A True

    B False

15 If you are having problems with your landlord where can you go for help and advice? Select two options from below

    A The housing department of the local authority

    B Citizens Advice Bureau

    C DVLA

    D A Primary Health Care Centre

16 When did twelve European states adopt the euro as a common currency?

    A 2002

    B 2000

    C 1995

    D 1980

17 What is the minimum age for purchasing alcohol?

    A 14 years old

    B 16 years old

    C 17 years old

    D 18 years old

18 How often are you required to take your vehicle for an MOT test if it is over three years old?

    A Every five years

    B Every two years

    C Every year

    D You only need an MOT test if the car has been involved in an accident

19 Who is given priority when GPs visit patients at home?

    A Children under five years old

    B Older people

    C People who are unable to travel

    D Pregnant women

**20 Independent schools are paid for by the state.
Is this statement true or false?**

    A True

    B False

21 Everyone in the UK is allowed to work. Is this statement true or false?

    A True

    B False

22 What is a 'gap year'?

    A A measurement used by the government to assess literacy

    B A period of time taken by a young person to work or travel before starting university

    C A year of study that has to be repeated

    D The first year a young person spends at university

23 Which of these statements is correct?

    A Employers have a legal duty to make sure the workplace is safe

    B Employees have no responsibility to work safely

24 Select the correct statement

    A It is illegal to employ children under the age of 14

    B You can obtain a special licence from your local authority to employ children under the age of 14

PRACTICE TEST 16

1   Which of these statements is correct?

   A   It is compulsory for children aged between 5 and 16 to attend school

   B   Children aged over 14 do not have to attend school

2   How many independent schools are there in the UK?

   A   100

   B   1,000

   C   2,500

   D   15,000

3   Which of these statements is correct?

   A   It is illegal to possess cannabis anywhere

   B   It is legal to possess cannabis in the privacy of your own home

4   What does Guy Fawkes Night commemorate?

   A   Remembrance of those killed during war

   B   The failure of a plot to bomb Parliament

   C   The invention of fireworks

   D   The rebuilding of the Houses of Parliament

5   In which year will the next UK census be carried out?

   A   2008

   B   2011

   C   2015

   D   2020

6   Who is the monarch not allowed to marry?

A   Anyone who is not of royal blood

B   Anyone who is not Protestant

C   Anyone who is under the age of 25

D   Anyone who was born outside the UK

7   When is April Fool's Day?

A   1 April

B   1 February

C   1 March

D   1 May

8   A judge can decide whether a person is guilty or innocent of a serious crime. Is this statement true or false?

A   True

B   False

9   The Council of Ministers, together with the European Parliament, is the legislative body of the European Union. Is this statement true or false?

A   True

B   False

10   What is a Life Peer?

A   A hereditary aristocrat or peer of the realm

B   A member of the House of Lords who has been appointed by the Prime Minister

C   Any person who has inherited a peerage from their family

D   Any person who has served as an MP for more than twenty years

11 **In which year were the Assembly for Wales
and the Scottish Parliament created?**

    A 1969

    B 1972

    C 1982

    D 1999

12 **Where is the European Commission based?**

    A Brussels

    B Geneva

    C Paris

    D Strasbourg

13 **In what year did the Prime Minister gain powers to
nominate members of the House of Lords?**

    A 1958

    B 1968

    C 1973

    D 1980

14 **When you make an offer on a home you want to buy, who is this
usually done through? Choose two correct answers from below**

    A An estate agent

    B A solicitor

    C A GP

    D A bank

15 What is the charge for the supply of water to a home called?

    A Income tax

    B Piping charge

    C Supply rates

    D Water rates

16 What are two stages that you must complete before you can get a full driving licence? Choose two correct answers from below

    A Pass a practical driving test

    B Pass an MOT test

    C Pass a written theory test

    D Pass a breathalyser test

17 What is the standard closing time of a pub?

    A 10pm

    B 11pm

    C 1am

    D 2am

18 Your car insurance will not be valid if you do not have a valid MOT certificate. Is this statement true or false?

    A True

    B False

19 You always have to pay a charge to receive treatment from your GP. Is this statement true or false?

    A True

    B False

20 **What percentage of children in the UK attend independent schools?**

    A About 15%

    B About 40%

    C About 5%

    D About 8%

21 **Select the correct statement**

    A Employers have to check that everyone they employ is legally entitled to work in the UK

    B Employers can employ anyone as long as they have a UK bank account

22 **How many weeks of paid holiday each year are employees over 16 normally entitled to?**

    A Five weeks

    B Four weeks

    C Three weeks

    D Two weeks

23 **Which of the UK national days is celebrated with a public holiday?**

    A St Andrew's Day in Scotland

    B St David's Day in Wales

    C St George's Day in England

    D St Patrick's Day in Northern Ireland

24 **What is the youngest legal age for children to do paid work?**

    A 10 years old

    B 12 years old

    C 14 years old

    D 8 years old

PRACTICE TEST 17

1   **What is the distance from John O'Groats on the north coast of Scotland to Land's End in the south-west corner of England?**

   A   Approximately 1,100 miles (1,770 kilometres)

   B   Approximately 1,310 miles (2,110 kilometres)

   C   Approximately 500 miles (800 kilometres)

   D   Approximately 870 miles (1,400 kilometres)

2   **What percentage of the United Kingdom's population is made up of ethnic minorities?**

   A   1.3%

   B   16.8%

   C   29.3%

   D   8.3%

3   **Who is responsible for investigating serious complaints against the police?**

   A   The Home Secretary

   B   The Independent Police Complaints Commission

   C   The Lord Chancellor

   D   The Police Commissioner

4   **How much has the UK population grown by (in percentage terms) since 1971?**

   A   2.9%

   B   23.5%

   C   34.1%

   D   7.7%

5 **What is the name of the ministerial position that is responsible for the economy?**

    A Chancellor of the Exchequer

    B Chief Whip

    C Home Secretary

    D Lord Chancellor

6 **When were women given voting rights at the same age as men?**

    A 1840

    B 1918

    C 1928

    D 1945

7 **Where can you get further information about welfare benefits? Select two correct answers from below**

    A A bank

    B A building society

    C Jobcentre Plus

    D Citizens Advice Bureau

8 **Where can you get a mortgage from? Select two correct answers from below**

    A A bank

    B A building society

    C An estate agent

    D A housing association

9 **What are the most common jobs that children in Britain do? Select two answers from below**

  A Work in hospitals or pharmacies

  B Work in kitchens

  C Work in supermarkets or newsagents

  D Deliver newspapers

10 **There are more women than men in Britain's population. Is this statement true or false?**

  A True

  B False

11 **Who should you speak to if you have health and safety concerns in your workplace? Select two answers from below**

  A Your supervisor or manager

  B The police

  C Your local MP

  D Your trade union representative

12 **In Northern Ireland, who is responsible for investigating serious complaints against the police?**

  A The Lord Chancellor

  B The Chief of Police

  C The Home Secretary

  D The Police Ombudsman

13 **There are no independent MPs in Parliament. Is this statement true or false?**

  A True

  B False

14 **It is legal for your employer to force you to work more hours than has been agreed in your contract. Is this statement true or false?**

    A True

    B False

15 **What is the difference in the average hourly pay rate for men and women?**

    A The average hourly pay rate is 5% lower for women

    B The average hourly pay rate is 10% lower for women

    C The average hourly pay rate is 20% lower for women

    D No difference – the average hourly pay rate for women is the same as men

16 **What should you do if you are involved in a road accident? Select two options from below**

    A Make a note of everything that happened and contact your insurance company

    B Give your details to the other drivers

    C Exchange your driving licence with the other drivers

    D Admit that the accident was your fault

17 **If you have a driving licence from an EU country, then you can only use it in the UK for up to 12 months. Is this statement true or false?**

    A True

    B False

18 **Most of the laws protecting people at work apply equally to people doing part-time or full-time jobs. Is this statement true or false?**

    A True

    B False

19 Who are welfare benefits not available to?

A The sick and disabled

B The elderly

C The unemployed

D People who do not have legal rights of residence in the UK

20 Choose the correct statement from below

A After a tenancy agreement has been signed, a landlord cannot raise the rent without agreement from the tenant

B A landlord can raise the rent, but only one month after the tenancy agreement has been signed

21 What do trade unions aim to achieve for their members? Select two options from below

A To improve their pay and working conditions

B Provide advice and support on problems at work

C To deduct tax from their earnings

D To limit overall pay increases

22 What percentage of children in the UK live with both birth parents?

A 25%

B 40%

C 65%

D 80%

23 After the age of 70, drivers must renew their driving licence for three years at a time. Is this statement true or false?

A True

B False

24 All dogs in public places must wear a collar showing the name and address of the owner. Is this statement true or false?

    A True

    B False

PRACTICE TEST 18: SCOTLAND

1   On which matters can the Scottish Parliament make decisions? Select two options from below

   A   Education

   B   Foreign Policy

   C   Defence

   D   Health

2   In Scotland, when do most young people take SQA examinations?

   A   15 years old

   B   16 years old

   C   17 years old

   D   18 years old

3   The Church of England is called the Episcopal Church in Scotland. Is this statement true or false?

   A   True

   B   False

4   What is the name of the established church in Scotland?

   A   The Anglican Church

   B   The Church of England

   C   The Episcopal Church

   D   The Presbyterian Church

5   In Scotland, when do most young people take Higher/Advanced Higher Grades?

   A   10 and 11 years old

   B   13 and 14 years old

   C   15 and 16 years old

   D   17 and 18 years old

6 **Where does the Scottish Parliament sit?**

    A Aberdeen

    B Edinburgh

    C Glasgow

    D Stormont

7 **How many Members of the Scottish Parliament (MSPs) are there?**

    A 105

    B 129

    C 158

    D 97

8 **At what age do children in Scotland go to secondary school?**

    A 11

    B 12

    C 15

    D 9

9 **Members of the public are not able to visit the Scottish Parliament. Is this statement true or false?**

    A True

    B False

10 **In Scotland, eye tests are free. Is this statement true or false?**

    A True

    B False

11 **Scots is the name of the old Scottish language. Is this statement true or false?**

    A True

    B False

12 **If you are buying a home in Scotland who should you approach first?**

    A A bank

    B A solicitor

    C An estate agent

    D Your local MP

13 **When is the national day for Scotland?**

    A 1 March

    B 17 March

    C 23 April

    D 30 November

14 **What is the population of Scotland?**

    A 1.3 million

    B 3.2 million

    C 5.1 million

    D 7.8 million

15 **The Scottish Parliament has powers to raise additional tax. Is this statement true or false?**

    A True

    B False

16 **What other regional language, in addition to English, is also spoken in Scotland?**

    A French

    B Gaelic

    C Scottish

    D Welsh

17 **In Scotland, when a home is for sale, the seller sets the price and buyers make offers below that amount. Is this statement true or false?**

    A True

    B False

18 **When buying a home in Scotland, a survey is carried out before making an offer. Is this statement true or false?**

    A True

    B False

PRACTICE TEST 19: WALES

1   What is the population of Wales?

    A 1.2 million

    B 2.9 million

    C 3.4 million

    D 5.3 million

2   When is the national day for Wales?

    A 1 March

    B 17 March

    C 23 April

    D 30 November

3   In Wales, free dental treatment is available to all people. Is this statement true or false?

    A True

    B False

4   Where is the National Assembly for Wales situated?

    A Cardiff

    B Edinburgh

    C Stormont

    D Swansea

5   In Wales, what is the name of the organisation that provides advice on careers to children from the age of 11?

    A Careers Wales

    B NHS Wales

    C Wales Connections

    D Wales EAL

6   Welsh is no longer taught in schools in Wales. Is this statement true or false?

    A True

    B False

7 At what age do school children take their first national test in Wales?

    A 7

    B 9

    C 11

    D 14

8 How many Assembly Members are there in the National Assembly for Wales?

    A About 30 members

    B About 40 members

    C About 50 members

    D About 60 members

9 On which matters can the Welsh Assembly make decisions? Select two options from below

    A Transport

    B Foreign Policy

    C Defence

    D Environment

10 At what age do children in Wales go to secondary school?

    A 11

    B 12

    C 15

    D 9

11 Members of the public are not able to visit the Welsh Assembly. Is this statement true or false?

    A True

    B False

12 At what ages do teachers formally assess children's progress in Wales?

    A 5 and 10

    B 6 and 10

    C 7 and 11

    D 8 and 12

PRACTICE TEST 20: NORTHERN IRELAND

1 Which of the following statements is correct?

   A Social housing in Northern Ireland is provided by the Northern Ireland Housing Executive

   B All housing in Northern Ireland is provided by the Northern Ireland Housing Executive

2 In Northern Ireland there is a system of domestic rates instead of Council Tax. Is this statement true or false?

   A True

   B False

3 In Northern Ireland the cost of water supply is included in domestic rates. Is this statement true or false?

   A True

   B False

4 In Northern Ireland, a newly qualified driver must display an R-Plate for one year after passing the test. Is this statement true or false?

   A True

   B False

5 In Northern Ireland, what are schools that aim to bring children of different religions together called?

   A Faith Schools

   B Integrated Schools

   C Joined Schools

   D Shared Schools

6 In Northern Ireland many secondary schools select children through a test taken at the age of 11. Is this statement true or false?

   A True

   B False

7 The UK government cannot suspend the Northern Ireland Assembly. Is this statement true or false?

    A True

    B False

8 On which matters can the Northern Ireland Assembly make decisions? Select two options from below

    A Education

    B Foreign Policy

    C Defence

    D Environment

9 The Northern Ireland Assembly was established with a power-sharing agreement between the main political parties. Is this statement true or false?

    A True

    B False

10 What is the name of the police service in Northern Ireland?

    A Metropolitan Police

    B Police Ombudsman

    C Police Service for Northern Ireland

    D Royal Ulster Constabulary

11 One of the dialects spoken in Northern Ireland is called Ulster Scots. Is this statement true or false?

    A True

    B False

12 When is the national day for Northern Ireland?

    A 1 March

    B 17 March

    C 23 April

    D 30 November

13 **How many members are there in the Northern Ireland Assembly?**

   A 108 members

   B 125 members

   C 64 members

   D 82 members

14 **What is the population of Northern Ireland?**

   A 0.9 million

   B 1.7 million

   C 2.5 million

   D 3.1 million

15 **When was the Northern Ireland Parliament established?**

   A 1922

   B 1938

   C 1945

   D 1956

16 **At what age do children in Northern Ireland begin secondary school?**

   A 11

   B 12

   C 15

   D 9

MARKING SHEET 1

	Test 1	Test 2	Test 3	Test 4	Test 5	Test 6	Test 7	Test 8	Test 9
1									
2									
3									
4									
5									
6									
7									
8									
9									
10									
11									
12									
13									
14									
15									
16									
17									
18									
19									
20									
21									
22									
23									
24									
Total									

MARKING SHEET 2

	Test 10	Test 11	Test 12	Test 13	Test 14	Test 15	Test 16	Test 17
1								
2								
3								
4								
5								
6								
7								
8								
9								
10								
11								
12								
13								
14								
15								
16								
17								
18								
19								
20								
21								
22								
23								
24								
Total								

MARKING SHEET 3

	Test 18 Scotland	Test 19 Wales	Test 20 Northern Ireland
1			
2			
3			
4			
5			
6			
7			
8			
9			
10			
11			
12			
13			
14			
15			
16			
17			
18			
19			
20			
21			
22			
23			
24			
Total			

SCORING GUIDE

Check your test results using this scoring guide.

Total correct answers	Grade
Less than 6	Very poor – Do not take any further practice tests until significant revision has been completed.
7–12	Unsatisfactory – Considerable gaps in knowledge. Further revision of study materials required.
13–17	Good – Not quite ready yet. Revise your weak areas to complete your knowledge.
18 or more	Excellent – Well done! You are above the pass mark and are now ready to sit the official test.